"Nancy Krieg's poems explore both the natural world and internal landscapes while paying close attention to the music of language. The resulting resonance echoes in the mind and in the space outside where sound takes them to new revelation. Read these poems aloud for their true effect."

-Shawn Pavey, *And Even if We Did, So What!?*

"Nancy Krieg's poems never fail to open themselves a little more upon each reading. These are poems of love that delve far deeper than the reflective surface of infatuation; they plow to the silt and bedrock of the nature of human connection, revealing the "heart's violent surge." The poems in this book speak to the cosmos within ourselves. Krieg finds the sublime musicality in our shared experience. Musica is certainly one of the many facets which show through in Krieg's verse. One moment you'll see "Monk climbing/ straight up to heaven," the next "Miles trumpet breathes/ in my ear." In the latter, the reader can feel the buds in their ears, see the monotonous cycles of the laundromat dryer, and experience the jazz genius transporting generations to more tolerable locales. While this book sometimes wonders if "perhaps we are the epitome of madness," above all, Cool Shades of Eventide implores us to always remember "you don't have to be strong, just human.""

-James Benger, author of *From the Back*

"It's been said that music is the healing force of the universe, I would argue that music is the thing that holds all of our existence in place. For Nancy Krieg in her new collection Cool Shades of Eventide, there is music everywhere. These poems ring like the banjo of sunrise, they hold the blues of time and look at its full face, they imbibe in the jazz of this now and they listen to the breath of the moment in all its tender cacophony. There is the alchemy of brush on snare while ride cymbal, clasp closed, sizzles around the sacred sound that only poetry can document. This is a fine book, a book of celebration and in her words Suddenly, we are all over the sky."

>   -Jason Baldinger, *A History of Backroads Misplaced*

"If *Cool Shades of Eventide* sounds like a blues song, indeed it should because professional musician Nancy Krieg penned this volume of poems containing many sketches from an insider's view of the music scene—from bluegrass ("John Henry," "Woodshed"), blues and jazz ("all good children," "Jazz at the Blue Room," "arc of the healer," "blue scapes ride till one," "keel over blues," and "Blues Round,") that includes a technique to motivate a fellow band member "because daddy needs his medicine" ("Todd Loves Nancy Drew"). One poem reveals insights to Janis Joplin's method of coping in "needle and the arm," and Krieg expands imagery by using visual art to describe music in "Eliane," who "folds clusters/of stars into square holes." Yet this collection doesn't solely explore music. Early in her writing endeavors, Krieg displayed both philosophical and psychological insights. Within the past decade, I have watched her writing evolve by weaving those insights into mysterious imagery, such as in "The Visitor" with a "suitcase full of torment/broken crown of stars/tangled in her hair."

>   -Lindsey Martin-Bowen, Author of *Where Water Meets the Rock* and *Crossing Kansas with Jim Morrison*

Cool Shades of Eventide

Poems by Nancy Krieg

Spartan Press
Kanasas City, Missouri
spartanpress.com

Copyright © Nancy Krieg, 2021
First Edition: 1 3 5 7 9 10 8 6 4 2
ISBN: 978-1-952411-63-2
LCCN: 2021936654

Author photo: Nancy Krieg
All rights reserved. No part of this publication may be
reproduced or transmitted in any form or by any means,
electronic or mechanical, including photocopying,
recording or by info retrieval system, without prior
written permission from the author.

Acknowledgments:

The author would like to acknowledge these publications who first published some of these poems online, in magazines, or anthologies. Thanks so much for the glimmers of hope.

Unfettered Verse: "I Imagine You," "adventures of a wooden indian,"
Ancient Heart Magazine: "invisible,"
Piedmont Literary Review: "The Kate in Question,"
Artistry of Life: "light traveler,"
Show and Tell: "songbird captured live,"
365 Days: A Poetry: Anthology, Volume 3: "blue scapes ride til one," "Solfeggio entrement avec Dolce,"

My work has appeared in these publications as well:

Lynx Eye, Lilliput Review, Voices: Poems from the Missouri Heartland, winedrunksidewalk, Soul Prints. a chapbook born at Kinko's in downtown KC

Table of Contents:

I imagine you / 1

love's mystery / 2

veils of the mystique / 3

kids at pond's edge / 4

slip into darkness / 6

dugout canoe / 7

invisible / 9

cool shades of eventide / 10

Logos, the word went wild / 12

matters of the heart / 13

Geisha / 15

farkeling with headgear / 17

Cooking Class / 18

perfect fit / 20

John Hardy / 21

all good children / 23

jazz at the Blue Room / 24

arc of the healer / 26

Woodshed / 28

Eliane / 30

Todd Loves Nancy Drew / 32

invitation / 33

blue scapes ride til one / 34

Mando Nando / 36

when the music stops / 37

Keel over blues / 38

same opera / 39

Blues Round / 41

sidemen on the sly / 42

songbird captured live / 43

needle and the arm / 45

the anarchist / 47

Solfeggio entrement avec dolce / 49

light traveler / 51

out of the blue / 52

spinning tales of gold / 54

intermission / 56

homecoming / 57

human / 58

where the curious roam / 59

firewater / 61

The Kate in Question / 62

my ego / 63

the visitor / 65

lost and found / 67

invention / 68

adventures of a wooden Indian / 69

Magic Theatre
For Madmen Only,

not for everyone
price of admission:

your mind

-Hermann Hesse, *Steppenwolf*

To my friends at 365 who share what they know and inspire me beyond all recognition. For all the poets, past, present and future whose kindred spirits keep us writing. To those who teach the craft, keep finding converts. If everyone could be a poet, think what our world would be like.

I imagine you

as the apex
of opaque, bright clouds blown
in azure skies silvered blue
gold coins your father gathered
align behind your goddess hair
trace light as they fall to earth
and treasure more
than siren song
worthy mates have
garnered from pirate stores.

perhaps we are the epitome of madness
but the feeling stays and glows
and it's real

beyond the gates
statues lost in verdant moss
like sacrosanct visions in clay
their form is pure and hardened art,
true hearts learn to give
the leery wake but once..

and once their death decides
wishes
and kings made of them
follies bleak
without eyes that see
the world with love.

love's mystery

outside, my neighbor's yard
seems a ticket
to higher ground
the iris, in lavender, cream
and dark violet risen on stems
tongues hanging like blood hounds
what becomes of them before the flower?
to describe the threshold mastered
before the ache desires to bloom?

awry, some horrid drips of hearts gone by
line drawings naked we
now aloof, regaled in truth
the painter's oils unveiled distortion
flowered anomalies, abstractions
as heart's violent surge
to be reborn.

the frame and matte
belie love's history;
and weapons use
to slice the seals
and tap the elixir?

always her mystery

veils of the mystique

slowly revolving
heart as prayer wheel
remember reunion
 rebirth child
arrow shot through time
she-mother, fertile warmth
desires wanton empires

memories   embers catch
junglemistinsidetearsofhealing
sacred beads of sweat
jingle streams

waterfalls
eroticAfricanprimalshaman
core of her soul, hersoul's
alchemy irons us into gold..
sacral gold from the core
of her being
she Goddess love
stratosphero moans
low clouds   heavy
thunder struck glow
new visions of an ancient world
veils of the mystique.

kids at pond's edge

at pond's edge cattails and pussy willows
caress the wind, in steel-blue, sun-warmed sky
your green eyes lavish love growing wild
in delight as you drink verdant scenery.
you pull stones from my soul
like stars shone in wounded night
skip them across in a side-slice hurl
five, six seven arcs as we watch
live art rippling in geometric waves
washing the pond-soul clear until
her surface is visceral and transparent.

you dive through its mirror
swim deep into the source
of profound, mysterious instincts
inside the peace of heart and soul
you rest, curled like an unborn child.
womb man, she is
my reason for completion
woman, she is
the depths of my intimacy
my blessings abound
you've appeared and you are real.

we are survivors, of cold dungeons
in kingdoms of loneliness
the taste, like joy and release of pain

sometimes, only tears
have the power
to diffuse life's emotional elixirs.

the warmth above your brow
marks your passage of escape
sealed tight with tender lips
you keep my soul from harm.

slip into darkness

on the vague side of my heart
I carve disillusions into
objects I can use: vases,
a rose for my teeth,
cool, clean mirrors,
images I recognize.

I know what light is
how it breathes life
into colors,   simple words
ignite the skies
of my mind.

if I were diamond-
flamed blue ice
convinced
of my worth

I would burn,
chase heartbeat
across tenderness,
tell secrets
until doves
disappeared   leave
the mirror empty,
fingertips intact
to braille the face
of another lover.

dugout canoe

two moons shine tonight
one gleams above
its reflection shimmers
projected below on river's screen
the curious eye of heaven and earth
as she watches herself, this quiet
array of rippled starlight cast across
luminous, liquid in slow motion
pulling stars apart, the tracer's lines
distort as she flows downstream.

to show you
how fast a dugout canoe
can travel the river
so deep, it's been carved
she moves light
and sleek-cut swift
among heavy laden logs
dense obstacles hidden
reminiscent of shallow lives.

sometimes
to feel the depth of space
where she's been gouged
forget the craft is there..
enter the space
where she is not
and yet,

that gives her form
my life becomes a rush run too fast
in despair and mistrust
falling, impaled by
some graveyard past
digging bones that pry
the stain and pierce
cold useless tears.

but she comes
to hold me near
like a child
she is night's
tender moon
and sparkled stars
her space,
we enter
her hand in mine.

Suddenly,
we are all over the sky.

invisible

to rise of wings, dance in the sky
art's fair loves make yielding souls
clear minds so bright in spirits' eyes
life circles, kindred, millions old
to celebrate ancestral match
from clouds, blue heart-found watchful gaze
souls' ancient rites from love's long past
bless bread of life for all our days
rare distance gone, one soft caress
be close, my harbored spirit's warmth
no touch to feel, false thoughts redress
blind image paints, yet has no form
real beauty dares not synthesize
to rise on wings, dance in the sky.

cool shades of eventide

mystique
loses her name
if revealed
saying everything
to everyone
the past becomes history
so many voices sanctioned
to recall feelings,
colored perceptions
that might have died.

emotions
we light them
like cigarettes and defile
the air of someone else
friends cough and choke
as they listen.

obscure
as the round stone
in stream's bed waves
distorted wallows wash
me into new overtures
the wait for solace
felt like winter's death
for a time.

I remember the coolness
the crisp newness
of beginnings
I keep it with me
a stone uncarved
is holy ground
the essence
of young love.

Logos, the word went wild

ego is an old coat wearing dust and self portraits
I've painted long ago
the unemployed actor waiting for audition
that might land the part
in tiger-tousled minions warriors
my Alexander, emperor
devouring everything in sight
he is the man who waits patiently
I constantly reassure, his time will come
I'll wear him when I must
he is sheer will and chivalry
love's raw power and desire
tamed to live by my side
could he become the vein
and not the shell?

Ego is the one telling this story
behind the looking glass
who imagined this monster
as the archetype to protect
this small frightened child.

Ego is the vein of human character
and without it's subtle fear
love has attempted to survive
on false gods and lies
without character
it's meaningless

yes, logos
the word went wild.

matters of the heart

when the wheel of life was set in motion
I was there, dividing time's
salt water strolls
in night's luminous glow.
I am crazy in love, relentless
as the moon moves tides
forevermore.

I know your fear as butterflies in flight
the beating of moth wings beside flame
the frantic tempo of love's desire
played in tandem.
one day as someone's careless faux pas slowed us down
you cry, "whisper me some tears, I've been shot from behind"
your guides replied, "you don't have to be strong, just human"
and I hold you until we find a steady rhythm.

I moved life through you father's veins
and mother's breast that first awkward day they made love.
I am the pulse that trickled red from the sacred palm
and if I chose a human form,
it would be the Christ
my labor being a simple act of love.

I understand more quickly than your soul
more slowly than your mind
whose insidious search for suffering
muddies my peace beyond recognition.

then I remember, my job is to be consistent-
I fold back in rhythm's pocket
and just keep time.
I am your heart
between every beat, I rest
and feel your love.

Geisha

In dreams awakening
to hurl among stars velvet skies
land in your cocoon
hold you like heaven is now
and forever, it shall be.
To sing love songs
in the key of this day,
play koto memories
shaped like your soul's veins
to unfold your heart
from foils of origami
until it shimmers
clean and newborn.

Quietly gaze into jade-saffroned eyes
embrace upon lips
tasting, ribbons pulled,
robes fall gently,
blind, braille of beauty
skin to skin
this revelation we explore...why?

Inside this overture
it all becomes clear-
I love you down to your soul
softly in afterglow, sleep entwined
there is no ending to our joy.

Butterfly, you are my wings unwrapped
translucent colors tracing arcs in sky
my love of freedom   flown away,
I feel you dream of your geisha
I will always come home.

farkeling with headgear

she is the one
to explore palatial celestial
adventures galore
galaxies drop their undergarments
space pure space
the great third eye
beams cyclopic waves over
a rainbow of gut wrenching
laughter.

yes, we could live on giggles,
she and I profusely, profanely
gleaned out of gelatin bowls
but our preference, is the mere
frivolous folly felicitously fed
casting of ideas into fishbowls
until we snare a big fish
to chew on. sweet rumination
of the fully eternal present
without the ugly bones.

Cooking Class

Down at Yung Ho the vegetables
do not survive son of Ginzu knives
chop-dice, cook-spice, evathing nice
on bed of luscious rice.

Impassioned pepperoni lie gracefully
amidst a sea of mozzarella and parmesan,
tomatoes shook from their vines
a lover's kiss from Giuseppe.

With wine to imbibe, the asparagus
mingle in a sea of Bernaise,
yolk to yolk, speak tarragon Francais
before they slip down the throat.

Juan Hose is a direct descendent
of Pancho Villa down Mehico way,
he put out the flame of
her chili rellenos
with his huge Corona.

It's evolution described
food took its partners
tongue in cheek, tangoed across
planet earth.

Ambassador for the Gods
food tames the beast of man
dresses him in lambskin bunting
catches him unaware.

perfect fit

the prelude: valid contemplation
stalking the gift of abandon
studying theory of relative warpage
smashing cloudbreast comfort
palms and fingertips mate.

in the land of less:
weight   effort   time
in a world of more is better..
we have more

morphed into the cosmic egg
sweet tear of universe eye
the yolk is running
ever so slowly.

John Hardy

on my way home on I 35
a billboard strikes my eye
a beautiful lady in Spanish motif
bathed in sparkling jewelry
the designer's name?
John Hardy

I hear the pick up notes
chime from JR's banjo
mandolin is barking
bass strum rhythm guitars
slamming down the tempo

Al picks a solo on guitar
sixteenths laced with chords
wearing his Tony Rice t-shirt
"I sent him an Al Hager t-shirt"
he notes with a grin

the music keeps running
the scene unfolding
amid the Cutty Sark pint,
beers and coffee cups
a bong named Merlin
keeps our synchronicity alive

John Hardy is just
a traditional tune
if you know bluegrass
but the memory...
still rings in my soul

all good children

Monk seemed to confuse other players
with his harmonic strides changing
keys more often than they understood
they disliked jamming with him
for fear of getting lost on a solo.

Compositions moved tonally into new
worlds, modulating across keys both
black and white, pounding gray
in diffidence with an ethereal
confidence he blew changes
and minds into the future
that too, was a syncopated reverie
rhythm from an unchained drummer.

I first met Monk in college as a music
major, in a small club where we'd play
jazz, a tune called "Straight, No Chaser"
the melody jaunts rhythmically within
the confines of a blues foundation

there's Monk climbing
straight up to heaven.

jazz at the Blue Room
for Pat Coil

there is no canvas
the scaffold scaled
in echelons far, uncharted
beamed into
other worldliness.

drummer paints amid
his color pallet
changing sticks and
brushes so often
you notice he's an octopus.

the pianist's composition
stuns me Zen for a time
I'm sure I heard every key
ring simultaneously
so long, I needed lots
of syllables for proof
of this effect.

the vibes player skips
mallet heads- reminds
me of a 1940's musical
humans dance across a giant
keyboard. "I love his voice"

spidery fingers
traverse the bass
seems like he's channelling
Bird, but no, it's all Bob
Salieri complains, "too many notes"
I disagree.

an impressionist painting
rendered in mystical air
by a four-headed genius
it's the gospel
I am luminous still.

arc of the healer

I recruited my doubts
trained my pet peeves
hand in hand
I brought my new family home
what a relief!
they sit on my shoulders
I hear them whisper
the smile starts
way down in my tummy.

I take my hide
to the art show
where dead artists
speak in healing
frame a la frame
my eyes drink
liquid hues in splashes
dead painters jive
the medicine man
rusted potions
but these, still alive
the recoil of a spirit
sprung by a friendly cobra.

the drummer sticks down the ice
sax man glides over
curves all points of light

into one coal train focus
hollow reed speaks rhythm
melts down tides of lava
swirled by the moon,
starry, starry sorrow
blew his mind
he warned us to get back
been through hell today.

Woodshed
poem for J.R.

in the back room
of our music store
his banjo chimes out
melodies of a song
as he tells me chords
I play along in rhythm
a novice mandolinist.

how did you get so good?
I ask when we break

came back from Viet Nam
didn't want to talk with anyone
took my banjo to the woodshed
and played every day
for nearly a year and a half
until the memories of war
became palatable and
the nightmares let go.

we played together
in our living room
each week for about
thirteen years, it was
our religion, and when
the last player left

my husband, Russ
and I sat in silence
bathed in vibrations
of sweet, healing
musical memories.

Eliane

the artists hands
soar like songbirds
weightless land on keys
blues angels trip into
paradise as palms flutter
summer breezes sway
so samba in her eyes.

she is here   she is gone
confusion tamed in sonorama
notes sky dive, loop and spill
in waterfalls on stage
beside her, she folds clusters
of stars into square holes
removes time, dis integrates form
to ride the joy of quietude
and build it all again.

some explode in destruction
quite Vesuvius a la improv
I care little if the hero won or lost
just want to hear the notes he plays
to see if they resonate.

she weaves a shimmer
around your soul   around
a kaleidoscope turning

as genius spins
the sky lights echo
songs from a heart of fire
and elegance.

Todd Loves Nancy Drew

after my drum kit is inside
I head to the bar for a beer
begin to set up
it's a Zen ritual
how each stand fits
each drum hangs,
the angle of a cymbal
one beverage is enough
to become relaxed and flexible.

I count the first tune
and its rough
the pocket eludes us
Drew and I tell Todd
"We think daddy needs his medicine"

he shouts to the barkeep
"Double Jack on the rocks"
and the edge we had
just before is gone
now we're striding down
Bourbon Street layin' back
Big Easy style.

invitation

she is
the samba train
round
coal fever
orange
light beam
ignores
the station.
steel
wheel smooth
one
focus
into fog
common heart
in a constellation.
belly
full of sol
stardust
glitter fall,
she feeds
passion fruit
drops the moon
in your arms.

blue scapes ride 'til one

it's so unique, an old store front
turned lounge, the musicians up against
the glass window-wall, just inside the door,
you could grab the neck of a guitar as it's being played
moving further would interrupt, so you sway in place
until the song ends, get a feel for the room.

it's the fastest call I've had at a jam, right now
Walker's up on guitar, that sweet old Gibson hollow
Lonnie owns and he sits down, cat hat slow
my shoes come off, pedal cold, high-hat gap adjust
there's a new singer too, he walks right up
takes the mike and control
I know he knows.

he kicks a shuffle and Walker digs in a slur tone pull-off
he loves that guitar, piled the wood in that shed
he's burning, just so his upper
soul could dream like this.

new tune
smooth, slow twelve plays me like a jazz waltz
then quiet like Otis meant what he says
I put in more back beat as they start to float
move them in close, strings like kites
as they tell me stories.

the dancers slice the air and inhibitions
more dips and swirls
than any ice cream parlor
in rhythm's time, their warmth is a blur
of cool art forming on the edge of life.

the owner hawks, last call, then it's one
they tear down the whole show
blue birds flying high
headed for a lounge in Omaha.

Mando Nando

because she spoke to me
from a recording I heard
and I fell in love, from Celts
to Italians, to Gypsy wanderers
she is famous worldwide
for the longings of her heart.

to the banjo man who taught
me hornpipes and reels
my nose in a book
learning to play on my own.

to untangle the lines of life
from a pile of useless strings
mandolins are so smart
they can teach anyone
to find their own song.

when the music stops

your sax wails a resonance
to time-out rhythms
haunts like primal, tribal scream
fury of sound bites chewing air
into near silence and chime ring
delicacy, the inspiration holds us there
bound in synchronicity
the feeling fades
we know when it's done.

when the music stops
your face goes flat and dim
recalls a grief held tightly
in helpless hands
the story telling you begins
it curves up my spine,
a tension revisited, arduously
described items you've packed.

the train moving past
deliver us from moments stolen
ground away in wheels rolling
one more chance missed
to spend your ticket
the bland, blank stare into space

I can't drive you to the station anymore.

Keel over blues

I can feel my heart shudder
like somebody ripped it out
and is shakin' it to death
ohh lawd some leftover anger
ahh the honey's gone dry
gooey mess on the shelf
plastic honey bear tumped over
roaches 'll be here
to eat him up
in a day or two.

But it don't matter
his heart's
done
stopped,

done stopped

while I was
singing this song.

same opera

Pagliacci. turns
my venom   cool   sings the
stones out of my soul.
blood letting,
fine   tune   balance
the virus you inhaled
escapes like Houdini
into thin air
like smoke
from a thunderstorm
let your eyes rain.

chain lightning
the fat lady sings
irresistible,
crescendo   absorb
artists'
energy

real time
it plays back
a recording layered
over nights of rehearsal
passion
perfection
inspired blur focused
stained glass pieces

divine window
streaming.

hearts pounding
we spring from monotone
prisons   out of time
shape shift
like sound bites.

Blues Round

my sneakers left
for the laundromat
where the ocean plays
on every tv set.

kaleidoscope colors
practice somersaults
Miles trumpet breathes
in my ear.

toes tap steady
and mean
clothes and soul
all fresh and clean

fade my blues
for a few quarters.

sidemen on the sly

on the Plaza, sitting at a
sidewalk cafe, the music's live
the trio is all cover tunes
suddenly my left ear discerns
harmonica with a rich vibrato
I turn my head, sure enough
my friend has pulled a harp
from his pocket and is playing along.
I clap right in his face,
because I can.

the ladies too, kept staring
at our dancer, the rhythm changes
and he grooves
like a diamond needle
on a hot new 45.

his creation did not stop
even found some moves
to jive with the folk/bluegrass band
we visited later on.

songbird captured live

three monks praying
on the dark
wooden floor, bar and
bottles streaming liquid
light   touch   amber
fingers no fret
easy blend walkin'
smooth piece of time.

zen drummer
mist covered
paint brushes the air
smooth transparent colors
black label rhythm, died
where the blank faces
shout from the deaf doorstep
quiet soul
don't kick no more.

pale notes run hushed
soft speak on nylon strings
hand over mind matters
scale the mountain of muse
swift blue green notes
into the clear stream
elixir of consciousness.

the songbird moves in
claps three, four
great ghosts shine
in her eyes, melancholy bliss
a long past comes down to this
moment of silk veils
cast at the audience
rides liquid amber waves.

fade and silence
palms flutter approval
like wings of nightbirds
stunned by a full moon.

needle and the arm

at Target in St. Louis
my cousin and I scan album
covers for art we like
OK, we're 12 years old
and don't know
an artistic cover might have
matching music inside
quite by accident we scored
"Inna Gadda da Vida"
one Saturday afternoon.

those frantic musicians on
"Cheap Thrills" hit a resonance
not to pass up. Big Brother and
the Holding Company
Janis Joplin on vocals
voice like a flesh wound
drummer echoes like
he's sitting in a clamshell
because it's live, tiny flubs
recall the lumps
in mashed potatoes
simply authentic.

a colleague said of Joplin
"Her sensitivity to the human condition
was so great, she couldn't stand the pain
and used heroin to escape."

sometimes those born
from the wounds
of the world
might use a needle
just to carry on.

the anarchist
for Jason Baldinger

he wakes with that ache in his eyes
doesn't need to find his brain
relentless rhythm begins
he knows it's a goddam poem

line one, middle, last
it does not matter
you can hear it when he reads
bam against the injustice he has lived
bam against the pain of others
freedom is the lament
of our captors

he is the June bug
bumping head against
the screen
leading you to the light.

he is a Quaalude flurry
of fireflies , a glow rising
rising from the cemetery lawn

he is the question
fate answers as circumstance
why else would injustice matter?

knowing burns like tenacity
he can light your heart
from the inside out.

Solfeggio entrement avec dolce

tonight I feel no moment's sorrow
and last, my eyes were veins
invisible ink no one noticed
the man in Chicago knows me well
as he paces streets toward train yard blues
drops light hellos as he walks
like a chimney, smoking.
He was my first savior
his reflection repeats itself
in half-lives etched
on sheaves of rain shining likechainmail
beautiful..

you are the river and its course
the bend in time and trees ceiling skies
the parabola continuum
courageously risk
your own sanity
each adventure opens wide
deluxe madness to share
blood trickles like red love,
read love, waxes the moon
mysteriously
there is no barter that matches
the immortal sound words create
as they blink from the mind
priceless..

we are sacrificed
sometimes even crucified
the lips of gods
drool a masterpiece
and we sleep like death.

light traveler

there are few doors left to open
that might shimmer in hope,
shadows pace behind you
in search of self-reflection
vague to each new threshold.

the tour guide is reluctant
to describe stars
that fall around you.
once, they burned high overhead.
now, traces of light impale
paths through your eyes.

the grief suffered,
the silence wished for,
folds its hands.
a quiet dawn encircles
like a warm embrace.

you remember,
stars seldom die
and look below
to see them
shining at your feet.

out of the blue

across the sky, she comes to me
in midnight's caress
I am startled awake
her eyes take me swiftly,
completely.

in moonstruck night, a world
of beauties sleep
quiet souls rest by day's end
the fire of existence calms
turns its face to the light.

she offers silence
plushed and rising Eden green
in touch of sky, spirits rise, rise
who have lived and died
she whispers to my heart
and lips begin to speak
the same songs
she taught the sparrow to sing.

she is the Eve's passion
uncarved innocence and perfection
mystique, beauty and curiosity
bared in the arms of love.

she is faint with shadows
only for the colors they choose
breathless falls on bended knees
in reverence to her lord
blossoms like the jungle
in foliage and sound
enslaves me in her paradise.

spinning tales of gold

grounded in the awakening
pouring elixir of gold
from the heart
tiny drops glissando like rain
emptiness, a useless
shroud to wear
as the souls listens
knowledge is the same
subjects over and over
an ocean tide of ideas
to wash the ghosts of doubt.

there is so much mystery
moving the scaffolds away.
open hands find freedom
so much darkness
inside every path,
the unknown grows less painful
as you accept blue midnight.
fears become trite
as you neglect time
and live on understanding.
light is moving
an element of song hums
in every space we dream.

it is the sound of the promise
the threshold
taking you into its arms
all the players come to call
who love you best
and know what you need.

intermission

I write to understand
chase my awareness
over blank pages
etch fear into lines
fold time inside envelopes
being born
we have wounds
holes in our hands
lids to close like eyes.

I've been inside
loneliness
for so long
I seem forgotten
hunted animal
I met myself on the road
declared my freedom
invited mystery to shoot me
make openings
where light can move
carve images
like iris blooming.

I tell myself
this is how the sky
won stars
holes in the canopy above us
the wounded night
shining in our faces.

homecoming

just yesterday
all my question marks
came home.
with them
I sit in the dark
ask them
of their journey.
they say it is a dream
in which every face
is our own.

we share silence
like prayer   happy tears
of sons home from war
bled in fears   healed in trust.
their arrival
is every wish I had hoped for.

old friends
the require of me no more than being.
what better love
than this?   to sit   sunk into my
soul   and they, being satisfied
to hear me say
nothing.

human

the reach is seldom faint
volition hurled through planets
new beginnings,   unborn
pieces of existence uncharted
ageless.   unknown.

the hunger of the spirit
seeks the Self   and Source
orbits   in parabolic missions
dies in breathless wonder.

imagined obliteration fails as
   solid, present,   opening
travails of light   enclose
captive stars   gleam
among shadows. fade..
    bend to listen
humbled in hints   of Self
   vague.   vacuous
subliminal   feather in time.

where the curious roam

tell me how the story goes.
blues shaken, not stirred,
a child brave enough to walk
right through crowd,
looks up, smiles
I stop searching
for God for a moment.
the travel is relentless,
lost count of the times
I've jumped the fence
the authorities don't ask
where I am going,
the rescue party appears on cue.

home seems more real
when I hunger or lust
for some idea or invention.
conflict plays on paper
in flash card images,
art is a vague song
of how life feels
until I tame the emotions
tell them from my own eyes.

sometimes,
I feel awake and alive
watching a river of time,

moments drift
like sheep counted.

asleep
I find places
to hide peace-
there is no where
to carry it home.

firewater

once the match loses its head
stand ready to dance in the fire
until the dream is over.

the lights on the water
flew like a sea of silver sparrows
dazzled my amoeba shaped eyes.
we must have looked like rainbows
from heaven way back then,
trapped in idiot-light, loving
androgynous cells of slavery
archetype of wind and feelings
reciprocal ecstasy from the Source.

earth is simply a magic show
Great Father and Great Mother
direct in virtual slow motion
friends and family appear and disappear
mysteriously after eighty years or so,
the fire of desire burns like genius.
there is more holy water
than the priests can claim.

I am one cell jangling in bliss
one cell pumping dreams
from its nucleus
into the sky
visualizing another
meteor shower.

The Kate in Question

She peers through jade colored eyes
until her mind connects
with unmitigated opinion
she squeals silently
like the Buddha
who has found the in-between.
The gems in ultimate question
gleam in half-life radiation.

Dark green bottles of Dom Perignon
explode such as this,
with fizzle and spark
glow in dark sides grin and quake.
While others steal
their light from the sun
she knows luminescence
is the mark of intelligence.

The genie's out of her bottle
high on brain waves
and hiccuping psycho babble.

Better catch her.
Green eyes flash, arcs of tracers
as she darts through the alley
on cat paws.

my ego

lives in a jar by the door
steeped in ancient holy water
deaf until the cap is unscrewed
and I have need
to summon arrogant powers.
I need him when I'm playing
supervisor at work.
he helps me play guitar
every morning during coffee.
and most important of all
he bounces on my shoulder in rhythm while
I play drums with the jazz band.

I never wanted to contain him, really
but he kept trying to run my life.
nearly drove me crazy
trying to keep up
with his unreasonable demands
taking himself so seriously
he wanted to run the whole show.

my soul was taking imagination rides
only to return
not knowing where she had been.
I never denied her the trips.
I was concerned, however, she would not find
her way back home.

down at AAA detective agency
you can get an overnight spy
for 59.95. great buy for a spy
and I did.
I couldn't keep my intellect
from following them
he watched her and the spy
all through the night.
my intellect trailed like a fox
recorded notes like a cub reporter,
sending the read to me at city desk
before they returned.
consequently, I never paid another 59.95.

my imagination is elated.
no more midnight interrogations ending
in tears and embrace of sorrow.
my intellect is happy with his job.
they take some wild trips together!
Me? I write down everything
that happens to them
and call it poetry.

now, my ego and I have a new hobby.

the visitor

she doesn't knock
just waits until
I answer
suitcase full of torment
broken crown of stars
tangled in her hair.
in my silence
she flows like wine
when I'm cool
she flies.

she lives on grains of sand
　savors time through this
　　hourglass mind
　in flesh of shells
the milk white bead
　her face?
mystery,　subtle shape
　new character.

a fog desiring order
she moves inside
images I define.

I recall days
of fire and ice
before she was born,

our eyes solving
an oracle of shadows
the promise of untamed dreams
we share in moonlight.

she holds the dawn in my eyes,
whispers sparrow songs
she is charmed ignorance;
I translate her soul.

pages   flutter   change
I leave the door open
so she can fly.

lost and found

there is no us
save the feel of rhythm
blind hands wave in the dark
do not believe in wings
instead, there are legs
useless feet to march
shameless to the difference.

the mirrors move faster now
everyone enters, a facet
of the jewel we carve together.
that mirror moves too
it bursts a caped crusader
out of the phone booth.

every soul crawls like water
moving to the unsung cadence
crystalline sun warmed
they shape shift in harmony
over moss and rocks.
emerald trees cast shadows
in blue depths inside
a crystal ball.

to define the wind?
   the hush
of wings
where angels move
our wishes.

invention

feather
hops a sparrow
soars through azure space
floats   into my hand
scratches a sonnet.

feathers down the chief's back
many silent people   courage
honor   brave feather
still traveling through time.

the Egyptians weighed the heart
against feathers.
a balance of sharing   we remember
pieces of time   love has
played between our eyes.

feather   scribbles across the desert
sky   new fables and blues go down
awakening   to lightness
clarity   wisdom
the voice of one soul.

adventures of a wooden Indian

remember.
fingers of lightning
cracked the rain open,
that day, half asleep
my map blurred, the rainbow
eluded me. in that moment
I already existed. all of
us are agents, you can't stop love.
the ink dried on the pages
before I could save any more ideas.

believe.
the man selling words
smiled and sold out last week.
he is mute by choice
still sits in his booth
shakes hands with people
who give him money
they appreciate
his candor.

honor.
we could be a myth of children
come to gaze in honest eyes
an arc of pleasure
moving between hearts
where silence of the mind
and presence of reverence
bears a beauty
beyond human description.

Nancy Krieg lives in Kansas City, MO where creating is cherished. She works as a job coach for developmentally disabled adults. She has been seen in jazz and blues clubs and sometimes art museums behind a drum kit, a djembe, or a mandolin. Now, she has turned her eye toward poetry because punching keys or even mandolin strings is so much easier than moving drums around.